AF373980

Start Here, Go There

Positive Affirmations to Start Any Day

Laura J. Peck

Start Here, Go There: Positive Affirmations to Start Any Day
Copyright @ 2020 by Laura J. Peck
All Rights Reserved
First Edition

To all my nieces and nephews,
life can be a challenge, but I promise you
if you always stay positive
your life will always be amazing and wonderful.
And know that I will always
be there for you no matter what
because you have given me the best
gift I have ever received and that is
your unconditional love.

"If there ever comes a day when we can't be together keep me in your heart, I'll stay there forever."-A.A. Milne

<u>Introduction</u>

In my book **<u>365 Days of Positivity</u>**, I used dates in relation to my positive affirmations. With this book, I decided not to use dates because I want you to start the first day on any day. I want you to have the freedom to start when you choose and if you want to start over on day one again, you have that chose.

When working to become positive, in the beginning we have this tendency to take quite a few steps back while trying to move forward. There is nothing wrong with that. I do not know how many times I took steps back more than forward till I finally realized the difference being positive was making in my life. It took time, but I have gotten to a place where being positive is a part of me.

From day one to day 365, you will be given a chance to change your life. We all want something better, but you must decide right here and now to go after it. We all get lost, but you can be found if you take that first step. I wanted something better, so I took action to make my life better. I was lost and after trial and error, I found myself.

Words only mean so much, but when you start to believe them in yourself, an amazing life is waiting for you at the end. I know this because I have and still live it every day.

To each positive day that you have in becoming you and living your amazing life,

Laura

<u>Start Here</u>

Day One

No matter what life throws at you, always be **confident** that you will get through it.

Day Two

Go out and see the sunrise. Go out again and see the sunset. How **breathtaking** it is to see the wonders of nature.

Day Three

Honor who you are not what others think you should be.

Day Four

Be **receptive** to that is all around you. Take it in, learn from it and share it so that others can become better just like you did.

Day Five

There will never be someone like you. You are a **rare** human being that was put on this Earth to do something amazing.

Day Six

Every second, every minute, every hour and every day is an opportunity to become a **new** you.

Day Seven

Believe that life is **simple,** and it will be.

Day Eight

Everyone around you is **blessed** that you are a part of their life.

Day Nine

You are **free** to always be the real you.

Day Ten

You can **accomplish** all the goals you have set for yourself.

Day Eleven

The **fire** you feel inside is the **fire** that will take you far in this beautiful life you live.

Day Twelve

Just as the sun **shines** bright when it is waking up, your heart and soul **shine** even brighter.

Day Thirteen

Your imperfections are what make you **perfect**.

Day Fourteen

Appreciate everything you have and everyone that inspires your life. Those things are, and those people are rare.

Day Fifteen

Life is an **adventure**. Go out and live it.

Day Sixteen

Be the **kind** person you wish everyone can be.

Day Seventeen

You are **unique** in every way possible.

Day Eighteen

There is nothing wrong with **caring** so much. It makes you special and whoever you end up with will be the luckiest person on this Earth.

Day Nineteen

It takes **courage** everyday to be you. Stay **courageous**.

Day Twenty

You are the **champion** of your world. Go win at life every day.

Day Twenty-One

How **stunning** is the beauty of your heart and soul.

Day Twenty-Two

Live a **magical** life as if you were a Unicorn.

Day Twenty-Three

No matter life's challenges be sure to always keep moving **forward**. One step is better than no steps.

Day Twenty-Four

Laugh as much as you can every day. It feeds the mind, heart and soul with life.

Day Twenty-Five

Learn how to **listen** to Mother Nature. Most of the time she has the answers.

Day Twenty-Six

Treasure those who make an effort to stay in your life. They are the ones worth fighting for.

Day Twenty-Seven

Enjoy life so much that you will wonder why no one else does.

Day Twenty-Eight

Know that someone out there thinks you are the most **wonderful** person they have ever known.

Day Twenty-Nine

Be **fearless** in going after your dreams. No one ever achieved their dreams without **fear** pushing them.

Day Thirty

Take time to be **quiet** and reflect on all that is you.

Day Thirty-One

You are more **valuable** to this world than you think. Keep doing you and you will see.

Day Thirty-Two

Your **ideal** life is the one you have dreamed of and imagined so do not ever stop seeking it.

Day Thirty-Three

You will always be a **remarkable** human being. Do not let anyone else tell you different.

Day Thirty-Four

Make an effort everyday to **brighten** someone's day. They will appreciate it more than you will ever know and so will you.

Day Thirty-Five

Be **inspired** to make a difference. For when you do, you will be **inspired** to do more.

Day Thirty-Six

Find the **calm** in all that is around you.

Day Thirty-Seven

Devote your life to you. Make it the best life you will ever live.

Day Thirty-Eight

Be an **original**. There will never be anyone like you.

Day Thirty-Nine

Life is an **experience**. Live it every day.

Day Forty

The best **prize** you can give yourself is by being you and living the life you want.

Day Forty-One

A **hug** is the best form of human touch that you can give to anyone. **Hug** often and long.

Day Forty-Two

Give the **best** of yourself each and every day.

Day Forty-Three

Get up each morning and **live** your life. It is the only one you have.

Day Forty-Four

Be **connected** to something bigger than yourself.

Day Forty-Five

The voyage you take today will bring you to your **destination** tomorrow.

Day Forty-Six

Precious are the ones that let you be you.

Day Forty-Seven

Have a **vision** that not only blows your mind but takes you to a place that you have always wanted to go.

Day Forty-Eight

Tell yourself everyday that you are **amazing** because you are.

Day Forty-Nine

Be **true** to your heart and soul.

Day Fifty

Unearth all that you were meant to be and watch your dreams come true.

Day Fifty-One

Tell yourself every morning when you awake that it is great to be **alive**.

Day Fifty-Two

Be **relentless** in your pursuit to always be happy. Being happy with who you are is the ultimate life.

Day Fifty-Three

Achieve a dream so big that you will not just stop there, but you will continue to keep going after all your dreams.

Day Fifty-Four

Cheers to you and all that you will become.

Day Fifty-Five

Teach others that they can become the impossible for the impossible is their dreams.

Day Fifty-Six

Your **value** to this world is bigger than you think. Go out and find it.

Day Fifty-Seven

Keep going. You are almost there.

Day Fifty-Eight

Hope is the one word that you should always believe in. It lets you know that life is so much better than you think.

Day Fifty-Nine

Always stay **centered** to yourself.

Day Sixty

Imagine the world you want and go make it happen.

Day Sixty-One

To **care** is to love.

Day Sixty-Two

Always look for that **twinkle** in someone's eyes. It lets
you know that they live life to the fullest.

Day Sixty-Three

Wisdom lies within all of us.

Day Sixty-Four

Nurture your mind, heart and soul with all the wonderful experiences that
life has to offer.

Day Sixty-Five

Always **donate** time to help others achieve their goals. When they succeed,
you succeed.

Day Sixty-Six

Envision a life worthy of who you are.

Day Sixty-Seven

The **best** is yet to come for you. Keep working on it, keep moving forward
and before you know it, it will be here.

Day Sixty-Eight

Say **yes** to you and your life.

Day Sixty-Nine

The **next** time is right now. Do not wait. Just go for it.

Day Seventy

You are the most important person in your life.

Day Seventy-One

Miracles involve belief, hope, destiny and you. Believe that they will happen. Hope they will happen. You are destined to have them and above all you deserve them.

Day Seventy-Two

Be **present** in every moment of your life.

Day Seventy-Three

Excel at life and see how amazing life becomes.

Day Seventy-Four

Giggle until it becomes a big laugh and watch how fun life becomes for you.

Day Seventy-Five

You have a **right** to be you and only you. Never change for anyone or anything.

Day Seventy-Six

You were **built** to handle anything life throws at you.

Day Seventy-Seven

Animate your life to be something so amazing that happiness is all that you become.

Day Seventy-Eight

Innovate a better version of yourself every day.

Day Seventy-Nine

Tell yourself every day that it is **great** to be just you.

Day Eighty

You have the right to turn the **page** in your book when you are ready to. Do not wait forever to do it.

Day Eighty-One

The voyage of **life** is yours to take.

Day Eighty-Two

Do not let fear get in the way of what you are meant to do so go out and take **advantage** of every opportunity that comes your way.

Day Eighty-Three

Open your heart and soul to only those who will take care of them.

Day Eighty-Four

Always **reach** for something bigger than you. Every time you do you get closer to your dreams.

Day Eighty-Five

Your **voice** lets other know that your words are true to who you are.

Day Eighty-Six

When you get up in the morning, you are already **winning** at life.

Day Eighty-Seven

I will admit life is not **easy**, but if you focus on the **easy** parts of it, it does become **easy** to live.

Day Eighty-Eight

Make it **clear** to yourself what you want and do everything you can to get there.

Day Eighty-Nine

Let it be known that you are **adored** every day by someone special.

Day Ninety

The **color** of your life will always be a one that makes you happy and beautiful.

Day Ninety-One

Always make a **deposit** into your own happiness. No one else can do it for you.

Day Ninety-Two

Always **quench** your thirst for life by going on as many adventures as you can.

Day Ninety-Three

When you find someone that gives you **loyalty**, hold onto it as tight as you can. **Loyalty** is a rare to find these days.

Day Ninety-Four

If you can **agree** on one thing, **agree** that life is the most amazing thing you will ever experience.

Day Ninety-Five

Feel the **upbeat** of life and dance with it always.

Day Ninety-Six

No **journey** is easy, but I can guarantee that if you focus on your happiness, your **journey** through life will be out of this world.

Day Ninety-Seven

Be **humble** in who you are and what you have.

Day Ninety-Eight

Rejoice in the life you have been given. It might not be perfect, but for you it is perfect.

Day Ninety-Nine

Plentiful are the riches of your heart and soul. Hold them dearly and do not just give them away. Those riches are precious to those who only see them for who you truly are.

Day 100

Be **generous** in what you bring to your life.

Day 101

Nourish your heart and soul with goodness every day.

Day 102

Life is about **fulfilling** your dreams. Do not let anything stop you from **fulfilling** those dreams.

Day 103

Always have an **appetite** for adventure.

Day 104

Relax, you are almost there.

Day 105

Every moment is a **teachable** moment. Always learn from it.

Day 106

Be **pure** in your intentions.

Day 107

Just **go** out and do it. Let nothing stop you from achieving your life.

Day 108

You are **awesome**! Believe in that.

Day 109

You must **motivate** yourself every day to do something amazing. No one else is going to do it for you.

Day 110

Some days are just about **being** here and that is all that matters.

Day 111

Make every day your day.

Day 112

Jump at every opportunity that comes your way. Even though it might not work out, there is always a chance it might.

Day 113

The most important person you must be **honest** with is you.

Day 114

Be **prepared** for something amazing to happen to you.

Day 115

Dazzle the world with your smile.

Day 116

The light in your eyes **gleam** the truth of your soul.

Day 117

Nothing is more **secure** than the love you give yourself every day. Make sure you do give it to yourself every day.

Day 118

Be **active** in life for life is too beautiful to sit around and watch it go by.

Day 119

When you learn to live the life you were meant to be, you begin to **bloom** into the person that was made to be on this Earth.

Day 120

Freedom starts the day you decide to be you.

Day 121

If you put your mind to it, you will be **unbeatable** at becoming you.

Day 122

Make the **choice** to get up every day and win.

Day 123

Visualize what you want and go after it.

Day 124

Be on a **mission** to succeed at life just by being you.

Day 125

It is **essential** to feed your mind, heart and soul of all things positive.

Day 126

Every moment you have should be **breathtaking**.

Day 127

We should always **unite** in love.

Day 128

Everyone has a **gift** that was meant to be shown. Go out in this world and show them your **gift**.

Day 129

Keep being **optimistic** that each day you are getting closer to your dreams.

Day 130

Devote every moment to be the **real** you.

Day 131

You are **worthy** dammit so do not forget that.

Day 132

Every morning hit the **refresh** button because you can.

Day 133

Rise to the challenge that is thrown at you each and every day.

Day 134

Agree to self-care for it is what will bring you to the next level.

Day 135

Jump on every opportunity that is given to you. It is an opportunity to learn about failure and winning.

Day 136

Send a **kiss** up to the sky showing thanks everyday for being here on this Earth.

Day 137

Set sail on a sea of opportunities that will change your whole world into a **wonderous** life.

Day 138

Self-care should be a daily priority. It is never to be put on the back burner for others.

Day 139

Dance in the morning. **Dance** at noon. **Dance** in the evening. **Dance** to the music that makes your soul come alive.

Day 140

Be **resilient** in every challenge you face because you have the strength to get through it.

Day 141

Experience is about living it and breathing it 24/7.

Day 142

Wherever you are you will always have an **anchor** with you. That **anchor** are all those that love you for you.

Day 143

Take the time to **unearth** the qualities that make you a human being.

Day 144

The **simplicity** of life awaits you.

Day 145

Gratefulness starts in the morning and ends in the evening. Do not ever forget to be grateful for your life.

Day 146

Feed your soul everyday by digging deeper into what your heart desires.

Day 147

When we take the time to **consider** what others feel and see, we learn not only more about them, but we learn about ourselves and how to deal with all human beings.

Day 148

Heal the voices that cause your spirit to question who you are and where you belong. Those voices are from the outside, not from inside your deepest core.

Day 149

Life is a **voyage** of ups and downs. Ride it with purpose, passion and your truth.

Day 150

Yearn for something so big that no words or actions could ever explain the true feeling it gives you.

Day 151

Someone will always be **glad** that they met you because you became a reason, a purpose, a meaning to their life at that moment.

Day 152

Believe that whatever is **meant** to be will be yours one day.

Day 153

You make the **medley** of your life. Make it resounding, beautiful, unforgettable, and beyond anything you could ever imagined.

Day 154

Set a **boundary** of love that lets others know what you are truly about.

Day 155

When you think you are not **ready**, you are **ready** for all the greatness that life will give you.

Day 156

Always give **one hundred percent** of you. The world deserves to see every bit of goodness you have.

Day 157

Be **willing** to show all that is you. This includes the scars because scars show our strength and our willingness to be vulnerable.

Day 158

You will always be **safe** in the arms of love.

Day 159

You are **plenty** enough so do not you ever forget that.

Day 160

Put your **trust** in something bigger than all of us. It knows who you are and what you are meant to be.

Day 161

It is **vital** to take a day to renew yourself. You have a right to recharge so that those who love you and you love always get the best of you.

Day 162

It is about **quality**.

Day 163

Rely on you.

Day 164

Now is the time to be your purpose in life.

Day 165

When you stand **upright**, you stand for yourself.

Day 166

Protect your **energy**. What you take in should always be positive, beautiful and hopeful.

Day 167

Dare to dream big because your dreams are worth it.

Day 168

Find the true **meaning** of your life just by being you and not what everyone believes you should be.

Day 169

The **light** within you will shine the brightest when you have found your purpose.

Day 170

Know this, you will always be loved. Do not ever forget that.

Day 171

In an **instant** your life can change so do not ever waste it on things that have no meaning to you.

Day 172

To be **happy**, you must find it within you.

Day 173

Give the gift of love whenever you can.

Day 174

Be the **friend** that everyone looks for and hopes for because there are few in this world that know how to be that one true **friend** everyone deserves.

Day 175

Nothing is more **exciting** than knowing you finally made it.

Day 176

Dive into life like there is no ending to it.

Day 177

Choose you every day.

Day 178

Always **believe** in you.

Day 179

Admire those who came before you and set a path for you to have the life you have.

Day 180

The **blueprint** to who you are lives inside of you and no place else.

Day 181

Go and **explore** the world you live in and learn how to make it a better, more peaceful place to live for all.

Day 182

Learn to **link** your heart and soul to those who bring out the best in you.

Day 183

Mother Earth will always **provide** for you if you **provide** it the peace, the healing and the love it deserves.

Day 184

When you **activate** your true superpowers that live within your heart and soul, all will be healed within you and around you.

Day 185

Be a **cheerleader** in someone else's life.

Day 186

The most **sensible** thing you can do for yourself is take care of you and always you first.

Day 187

The **oasis** of your heart and soul is where you always find peace and solitude. Let that be the way to happier life.

Day 188

When you write your story, make it a **novel** that shows all your flaws, all your mistakes, all that made you strong, all the love you gave and all that is you. Your **novel** is bigger than life itself.

Day 189

Plant love all around you and watch it grow.

Day 190

You have the **skill** to do anything you want. You just must go out and show it.

Day 191

The one that belongs to you will always be **captivated** by your big heart, your unwavering soul, but most of all by your beautiful smile.

Day 192

Maintain the peace you deserve in the world that surrounds you.

Day 193

Exquisite is the beauty that lies within you that most miss out on because they can only see the outside of you.

Day 194

Remember what it was like to be free when you were young? It was called having **fun** everyday of your life. Do not change that as you become older. Live a **fun** life every day.

Day 195

Be a **giving** human being.

Day 196

You are the **one** true you.

Day 197

Transform your life each day you get up and never stop until you get to you.

Day 198

Paradise is right outside your door. Feed it with all the love you have in your heart.

Day 199

Victory is in your corner.

Day 200

Be a **classic** in a world of modern.

Day 201

You have the **strength** beyond anything to get through any challenge you will face throughout life.

Day 202

To be **brilliant** at life, you must be willing to learn each day of your life.

Day 203

You must be the one to water your **garden** of knowledge. No one else will do it for you. Others will teach you, but you must be willing to learn.

Day 204

The **seed** of infinite and true love resides deep inside your soul.

Day 205

I am **absolutely** positive that you will make an impact on this world.

Day 206

Just be **brave**.

Day 207

Congratulate yourself for making this far in a world that sometimes builds walls to stop you. You broke through many walls and will break through many more.

Day 208

Distinguish yourself from others. You are like no other and will never be.

Day 209

Welcome to a life that will never be the same because you are here.

Day 210

Look **up** to the sky and say thank you for a beautiful and magical life.

Day 211

Each day you do something that puts you closer to your dream, consider yourself **growing** into the person you want to be.

Day 212

Always listen to your gut **instinct**. It knows.

Day 213

One's **heart** is a magical entity that lets us see how love can change not only ourselves, but the world around us.

Day 214

When you put the **effort** in every day, you will begin to see that the small results will eventually bring all that you have been seeking.

Day 215

It is **fair** to say that you belong here on this Earth to do something out of this world.

Day 216

Progress in any form starts with you. What are you waiting for?

Day 217

To become **whole**, you must search within and let go of fear.

Day 218

Seek **knowledge** every day and you learn to become the person you seek.

Day 219

Celebrate the life you have been given. It might not be easy at times, but when it is amazing, **celebrate** it.

Day 220

Be **unwavering** in your decisions because those decisions could one day change your life.

Day 221

Find **harmony** within yourself when you walk with nature.

Day 222

The **bountifulness** of life is all around you if you just take a step back and breathe it in.

Day 223

Accept that some things will not happen, will not work out and just let it go. You will realize one day that it was not meant for you.

Day 224

Find the **sparkle** within you that shines on a life you deserve.

Day 225

Learn to love with everything you have. The world needs it and wants it. And so do you.

Day 226

The world is **lucky** to have you. Believe that.

Day 227

Restore yourself by being out with Mother Nature. The trees, the grass, the sand, the dirt, the clouds, the sun, the water, the moon and everything She has will give you everything you need to be yourself again.

Day 228

Your **vibrant** soul wants you to live a life of purpose. Go out and do it.

Day 229

Nature is my home and I will seek it every day.

Day 230

Your purpose is to live a **meaningful** life. Do not ever forget that.

Day 231

It is **okay** to have days that do not feel **okay**. Just remember that in that moment, you do not have to stay there. You can move from it and let it go.

Day 232

There is an **elegant** dance we all do. I hope you will always do it like no one is watching.

Day 233

Every day is a **fresh** chance to begin again. Remember that.

Day 234

The **spiritual** being within you is seeking the true you.

Day 235

You are **intelligent**, beautiful, amazing, loved and so much more. Pass it on.

Day 236

Your **personality** is what draws people to you. Show them how to show off theirs.

Day 237

Do not be **quick** to assume. Take the time to learn and find the truth.

Day 238

How **terrific** it is to know that you are one unique and special human being here for an amazing reason.

Day 239

Have such a **zest** for life that regret eventually does not exist in your vocabulary.

Day 240

Be **strong** in your pursuit to live a life of purpose.

Day 241

Know that your life will be **legendary**.

Day 242

No one can imitate who you are or make a **Xerox** copy of you. You are one in a zillion.

Day 243

To see your true life and get what you want, it must be **vivid** in your mind.

Day 244

No matter the obstacles, the walls in front of you, the everyday challenges, you must get up and **persevere** every day.

Day 245

Be **mindful** of what you say to others. It should always come from love.

Day 246

When you accomplish a goal, you have every right to be **giddy** and celebrating it. It is your right to show happiness in this.

Day 247

Invent a life you can be proud of.

Day 248

To be **healed** is to know that you found the true meaning of love and why it is so important.

Day 249

To take risks that can change your life, is to be **bold** in your decisions.

Day 250

Be **wealthy** in knowledge that will not only change your life but will change others.

Day 251

Observe your life and make the changes necessary to make it amazing.

Day 252

Kudos to you for making it this far. You will get there; I promise you that.

Day 253

You are **qualified** to be part of this amazing world just by being you.

Day 254

To be part of this life is a **thrilling** ride you do not ever want to miss.

Day 255

To help others is the highest **noble** deed you could ever do.

Day 256

Receive what is meant for you.

Day 257

What a **joy** it is just to be here in this moment.

Day 258

Keep going because you are about to **flourish** in a world that wants you.

Day 259

Nothing can be more **adorable** than your smile. Share it often.

Day 260

You have such a **zeal** for life that others want to always be a part of it.

Day 261

Nothing is more **eloquent** than the beauty of your heart and soul.

Day 262

You are a **delightful** and amazing human being that belongs here.

Day 263

Life is a **cabaret** so keep on dancing to it.

Day 264

Get into the **zone** each morning to take on the day and smash it.

Day 265

Life can be like an **ultra** marathon but know that you can finish it each day.

Day 266

Make the **upgrade** to a better life.

Day 267

Look beyond the **horizon** and see what is truly possible.

Day 268

Life is **delicious** in a way that there is always sweetness around you.

Day 269

Be **persistent** in loving yourself every day.

Day 270

You are a **superb** human being so do not ever forget that.

Day 271

Make sure that in everything you do, you give it all the **gusto** you have.

Day 272

Your **health** whether it be physical, mental, emotional or spiritual should always come first in all that you do. You take care of you first and everything else will fall into place.

Day 273

Be **zany** every once in a while.

Day 274

You do not ever need **validation** from anyone to know what is right for you. Your heart and soul know what is right for you.

Day 275

Now is your time. What are you waiting for?

Day 276

Be **cool**.

Day 277

Isn't it **fascinating** that we get to live a life that lets you be you? I think it is beyond amazing.

Day 278

Here is the deal…. you are your own **truth** so do not let anybody tell you anything else.

Day 279

This **enormous** and grandiose life is yours to take and make the most of so go out and grab it.

Day 280

You are **capable** of doing the thing you are passionate about. This is your purpose so go out and do it.

Day 281

Be **healthy** in the choices you make. You are the only one that can truly take care of you.

Day 282

You are **gorgeous**.

Day 283

Discover your heart. **Discover** your soul. **Discover** you.

Day 284

Be the one that **uplifts** everyone else for then you will also **uplift** yourself to the highest of being.

Day 285

Find the **youthful** part of you that still exists so that you can remember the freedom you once had and can still have again.

Day 286

How **irresistible** it is to just be you.

Day 287

Nothing is more **fabulous** than that smile of yours. Show it and be proud of it.

Day 288

Be **truthful** in not only your words, but your actions.

Day 289

The true, **energetic** source of you is felt by all. Use it for kindness, good, hope, but most of all love.

Day 290

This **radiant** fire you feel inside is your passion wanting to be seen.

Day 291

Show off those **jazz** hands as much as possible.

Day 292

Compose your own music to the beat of the life you want to life.

Day 293

We are **quirky** in our own way.

Day 294

Superpowers are within you.

Day 295

Be **well** always.

Day 296

Make sure you make your life **user-friendly** every single day.

Day 297

Be **fortunate** that you get to live a life with Mother Nature. Her beauty is unmatched by anything else. Treat her with unwavering respect.

Day 298

You can find **heaven** within you if you choose to open your heart and soul.

Day 299

We all have **kindred** spirits around us. You just have to let them in.

Day 300

You must keep **moving** forward to become the version of you that not only the world wants, but your heart and soul knows is your truth.

Day 301

Be so **good** to you that you will know how you should be treated by others.

Day 302

Bravo to those who continually wake up to their selves in light of life's challenges.

Day 303

The greatest wonder in **life** is to live it, see it, thrive in it, enjoy it, be grateful for it and walk in its world.

Day 304

There will be only one of **you**.

Day 305

Reward yourself with a life that is beyond your wildest dreams.

Day 306

When you have purpose and passion, life is **effortless** because you are living the life you want.

Day 307

Being **powerful** not only means you are lifting yourself up, but you are lifting others up to their highest potential.

Day 308

Your heart and soul are the **vault** to the most magnificent person you will ever know. That person is you.

Day 309

Be **dazzling** in everything in you do. In other words, bedazzle your life.

Day 310

It is so **neat** to live in a world where your dreams, your goals, your passion and your purpose can come to life. You must choose it first and foremost.

Day 311

On this one, all I can say is "**Yay!**"

Day 312

The biggest **achievement** you can have is to live your life your way, doing what you love and loving the people that truly love you for who you are.

Day 313

Tell this to yourself every day, "I will **thrive** in this life that I was given no matter the challenges for I am important to this world."

Day 314

Being **independent** from the world is the most amazing thing you can do for yourself. You do not always have to be dependent on it. Learn to be self-sufficient and see another side of yourself you have never known.

Day 315

Zappy is how I am going to be today, tomorrow and the next day.

Day 316

Make yourself a **priority**. It is that simple.

Day 317

Earth is your playground so always make sure you go out to visit it, enjoy its beauty, reconnect to its energy and love it like there will never be another.

Day 318

Craft a life that allows you to be free in all that you do.

Day 319

You do have a **heart** of gold that is worth more than anything else in this world.

Day 320

Life is a **timeless** piece of art we get to draw on every day.

Day 321

Keep **returning** to you.

Day 322

Today is your day.

Day 323

I want to see that beautiful **smile** of yours every day.

Day 324

Any time you take a step back, it is not a failure, but an opportunity to learn from it. Life always has an answer. You must stop, listen and see the **lesson**.

Day 325

We are all **human**.

Day 326

It will take any **length** to become the person you want to be. Do whatever it takes no matter how many times you fall.

Day 327

Make sure you are **investing** more on yourself than anyone else. You are the most important person in your life.

Day 328

Be your biggest **fan**.

Day 329

Declare everyday your day.

Day 330

We are all **interconnected** as human beings. We have all that is needed inside of us to be one.

Day 331

There is so much **beauty** around you. Go out and enjoy its true benefits of healing and renewal.

Day 332

To **venture** out in this world, is facing all your fears to live your life the way you want.

Day 333

Take time to **visit** the ones that believe in you, that truly love you, that know you are special and unique and see the spirit of life through you. It is rare to have those kinds of people in your life.

Day 334

Your time is **now**. Do whatever you can to get to you.

Day 335

You have the right to **rest**. This is your body, your mind, your emotions, and your spirit telling you it is ok to stop for a moment and recharge so that you are ready for your next step.

Day 336

The **world** is yours to take and make an amazing life from. You must go out and do it.

Day 337

Once in your life you will make a **connection** with someone that will change your life forever. Do not force it, do not rush it, just let it be and it will happen.

Day 338

It has always been **obvious** that you are the most amazing human and you are meant to do something amazing. Always believe that.

Day 339

Only the **wise** know that happiness comes from within. Stop looking for it on the outside.

Day 340

Your life will always be an ongoing **quest** to live a life of purpose and passion.

Day 341

Some days you just need to **jam** out loud.

Day 342

Marvel at the beauty that is all around you and within you.

Day 343

You have the right to scream "**Yippee**!" has much as you want.

Day 344

Know for certain that someone out there **supports** you in finding your passion and purpose. Go out and do it.

Day 345

Astonish in the wisdom that comes from within you. It has always been there.

Day 346

When you go to your **Zen** zone, take this thought with you, "You are here are for a reason. You are meant for something bigger. There is a purpose for you. Believe that."

Day 347

The **glitz** and glamour of life is not found on the outside. It is found inside you. Show it off to the world and let them know how it is done.

Day 348

Dream big **dreams** because when you put in the work, they will come alive.

Day 349

Be so **passionate** about one thing that your life from that day will never be the same. That one thing will become your purpose. That purpose will become the best thing to ever happen to you. That best thing will be the life you have always wanted.

Day 350

Wake up every morning living a **fantastic** life.

Day 351

I can **assure** you that going on adventures will be the most beautiful, amazing, wonderful thing you could ever experience.

Day 352

You are a **jewel** that can never be replaced.

Day 353

Zoom into life like there is no other.

Day 354

How **quickly** life can go by. But, if you live in the moment each day, it will last forever.

Day 355

Utilize your time wisely to learn something new and to live your life the way you want.

Day 356

Find the **oneness** that connects you to something bigger than what you see in front of you.

Day 357

Just like a tree, a flower or even a weed that grows through a crack in the sidewalk, you are capable of **blossoming** through the challenges of life into something beautiful.

Day 358

Having an **empathy** for others is a superpower to understand how the world needs to heal. The first person to start with is yourself.

Day 359

This world is full of beauty, love, wonders and so much more that you should wake up **mesmerized** every day by it all.

Day 360

We all have some **nifty** skills that could make this world a better place. You must decide to go out and show them off.

Day 361

There is nothing wrong with acting like a **kid** every once in a while.

Day 362

Every day is a **great** day to live on this beautiful landscape we call Earth.

Day 363

Live everyday **like** it is the first.

Day 364

To be **young-at-heart** is to live a life of fun, excitement and adventure.

<u>Go There</u>

Day 365

The **universe** will always be there to show you the way.

www.ingramcontent.com/pod-product-compliance
Lightning Source LLC
Chambersburg PA
CBHW051503140726
47987CB00006B/2857